# Let's Play I SPY St. Patrick's Day!

honey sprouts

# NUMBERS

1 2 3 4 5

6 7 8 9 10

CAN YOU COUNT TO 10?

# COUNT TO 1

## 1 DONUT

**1**
........
**ONE**

# COUNT TO 2

## 2 RAINBOWS

**2**
· · · · · · · ·
**TWO**

# COUNT TO 3

## 3 LEPRECHAUNS

**3**
......
**THREE**

# COUNT TO 4

## 4 UNICORNS

**4**
............
**FOUR**

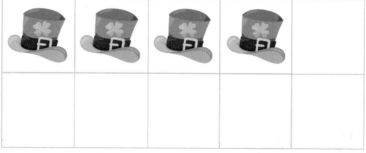

# COUNT TO 5

## 5 PIRATES

## 5
### five

# COUNT TO 6

**6 KIDS**

**6**
······
**six**

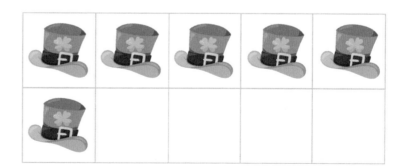

# COUNT TO 7

7 CUPCAKES

7
seven

# COUNT TO 8

8 Foxes

8
........
eight

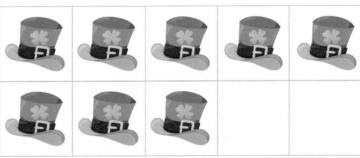

# COUNT TO 9

9 OWLS

9
nine

# COUNT TO 10

## 10 CLOVERS

### 10
#### TEN

# COLORS

# WHAT ARE THESE COLORS?

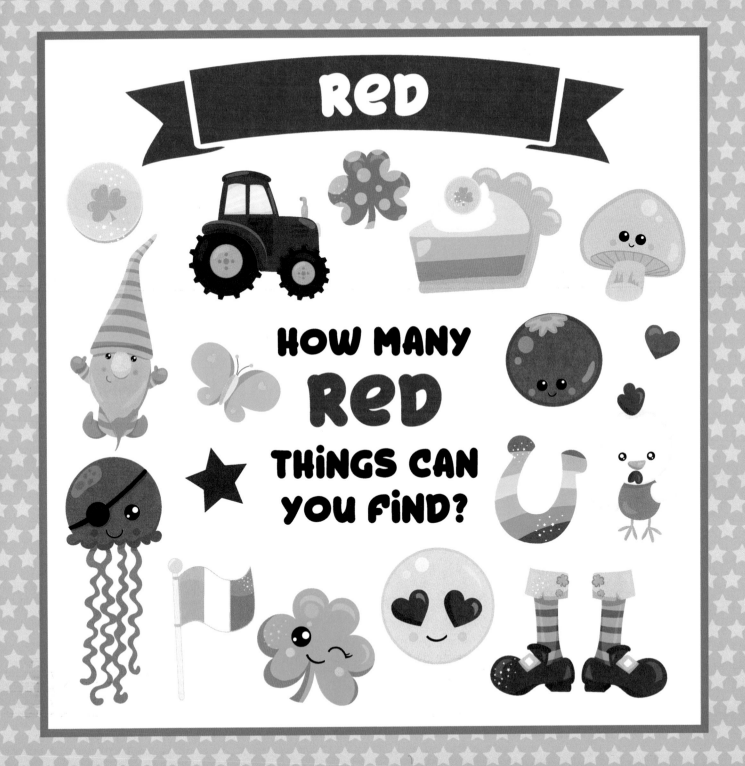

# BROWN

## HOW MANY BROWN THINGS CAN YOU FIND?

# BLACK / GRAY

## HOW MANY BLACK OR GRAY THINGS CAN YOU FIND?

# SHAPES

## WHAT ARE THESE SHAPES?

# SQUARE

 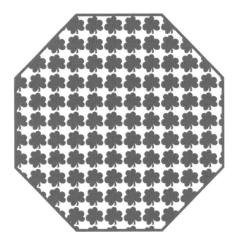

**FIND THE SQUARE**

# CiRCLE

# TRIANGLE

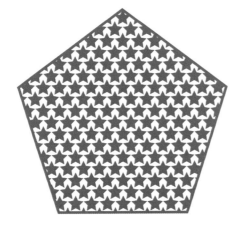

FIND THE TRIANGLE

# pentagon

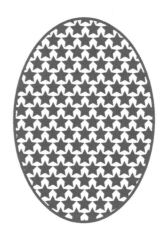

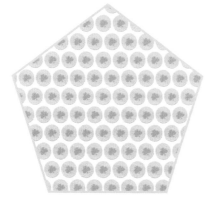

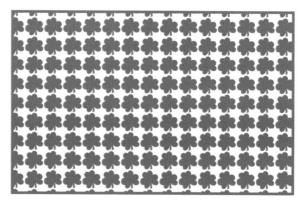

 **FIND THE PENTAGON**

# STAR

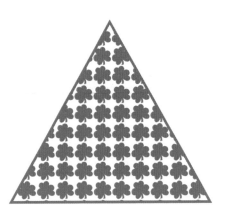
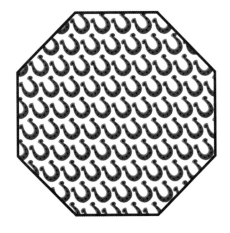

 **FIND THE STAR**

# HEXAGON

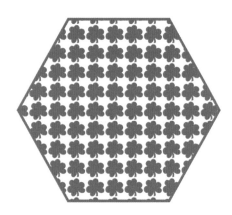

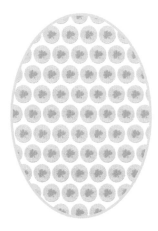

 **FIND THE HEXAGON**

# OCTAGON

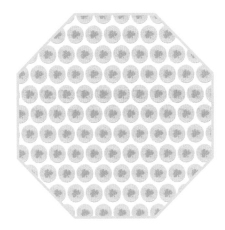
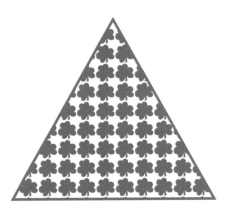

 **FIND THE OCTAGON**

# OVAL

 **FIND THE OVAL**

# RECTANGLE

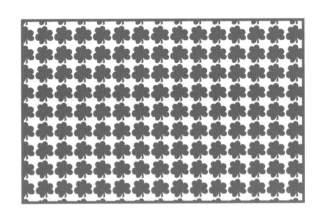

## FIND THE RECTANGLE

# DIAMOND

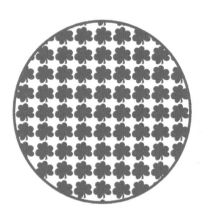

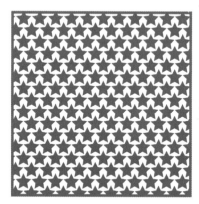

 **FIND THE DIAMOND**

# i spy

# FIND THE HIDDEN ITEMS

# CAN YOU FIND:

**3 COINS**

**2 UNICORNS**

**4 HEARTS**

# CAN YOU FIND:

**2 SHARKS**

**3 FRUITS**

**3 BALLOONS**

Made in the USA
Coppell, TX
10 March 2021